Caught in the Eye of the Storm

Third Printing

Tracy Flaggs

Caught in the Eye of the Storm

Tracy Flaggs

PUBLISHED BY:
BRENTWOOD CHRISTIAN PRESS
4000 BEALLWOOD AVENUE
COLUMBUS, GEORGIA 31904

Dedication

This book is dedicated to God Almighty whom I live, move and have my being in. With God, I am more than a conqueror and I can do all things. Without God, I am nothing. Oh how excellent is my God! His mercies are new everyday and he is able to do exceedingly abundantly all I could ever think, hope or imagine. Absolutely nothing is impossible for the miracle working power of God. I thank you, Lord, for allowing me to be a walking miracle! I give you all honor, glory and praise for healing me and making me whole! Truly, I serve an awesome God!

I also dedicate this book to my Grandparents who have had a tremendous impact on my life.

Grandma Bowie, Gram (My Sweetie) and
Gramps (Cuppie)

Thank you for your unconditional love! You paved the way and lead by example. Now your spirits live forever in my heart.

Contents

Acknowledgments

I want to acknowledge those who journeyed with me. Those who stood strong when I could not. The list of people is too long to name one by one…the display of God's love in my life was unlimited. Nonetheless, wisdom dictates that I name as many as I can:

Brian and Marian Flaggs

You are truly one in a million!
You are the best brother and sister
in the whole wide world bar none.
I love you.

Ariel and Alyxis Flaggs

My cupcakes!
Thanks for expressing your true feelings
and teaching me to express mine.

Nathaniel Adams
Thank you for your devotion to my health and to
caring for me during a traumatic time in your own life.
Thanks for making me a priority when I needed you.
I will always be grateful.

Love ya,
Shortie

My doctors, my surgeon and home nurses.

The hospital staff at both McLaren Hospital and The Cleveland Clinic Foundation.

Thank you for caring for me with patience and love.
Even in the most critical moments,
you didn't give up on me.
You prayed for me, cried with me, coached me and nursed me back to health. You tried everything humanly possible and then you allowed God to use you for his glory.

To those known and unknown who prayed with and for me, thank you.
The prayers of the righteous avail much.

My **family** who constantly shower me with unconditional love:
My dad: **Leo P. Flaggs**
My adoptive parents: **Rev. and Mrs. Roy A. Allen, Sr.**
Chuck and Rev. Dr. Linda Hollies

My God parents: **Daddy Yates, Hope Smith, Sylvia Wheeler**

Mildred King (Aunt Mil)
Richard and Ruth Smith
Ann and Joe Marshall
The Bowie Families
The Chapman Family
Ella Flaggs, Johnnie, Saundra
Marsha Flaggs, Gail, Diane
Earl II
Mr. and Mrs. Reid, Delores Reid
Mrs. Henry, Mrs. Braddock, Daisy Evans
Mrs. Miller Watts, James Anderson, Linda Moore
and my entire extended family

Tara Williamson, Paulette Wilcox, Mae Joyce,
my sisters who cried along with me in the midnight hours

Daisy Belle Quinney, Vernell Jones, Maxine Cain,
Ann Paquet, Pat Chunn
who tenderly and lovingly nursed me back to health.

Brenda Lewis who kept me sane during insane times,
Thank you for being my lifeline.

The Cass Tech Breakfast Club:
Lenora, Kristy, Gabe, Stephanie, Pat, Sara
who helped me laugh when I wanted to cry.

My buddies and adoptive brothers:
Tam, Stephen Clifford, Lonnie Lee, Derrick Williams,
who have given me the gift of true friendship.

My professional family and work connections:
my boss, my mentor and my friend and all those who allowed God to use them to testify that God's promises are true…
"God will supply your every need."

R. Burgess
Thanks for being my surrogate father, teacher and coach.

Geraldine Ford Brown
Who makes the best banana pudding!

Ronda Dunson, Terrye Garrett, Jerome Huddleston,
The Miller Family
(Duane, Diane, Audra, Tiffany), Karalee Tabron,
Lynn Scully, Francy Lucido,
Rose Daniels, Doris Hall
and many, many more who called, came by, sent
flowers, cards, letters of encouragement and lots of support:
Thank You All.

My spiritual families at both
Chapel Hill Missionary Baptist Church and
Word of Faith International Christian Center

My church mothers and dads
Kenneth and Deborah Dixson
Mrs. Emma Hudson
Shirley Morris

My prayer warriors in **Word Cell Group**
and **Sister Allie Paige**, my intercessor

Those who encouraged me to write and tell my
story of God's miracle working healing powers

Patsy Corniffe
Thank you for the perfect storm picture!

Caryn Jaeger and **Belinda Miller**
who have been midwives in the birth of this book!

Foreword

This is one of those "Lord, I can feel the sista" books! For with great emotional sacrifice, deep spiritual reflection and tremendous strength and courage, Tracy takes us with her on her personal journey to hell and back. This is one of those, "My God, how could she take it?" books! For God's best design for Tracy has her starting in "down", moving on up and then spiraling down, again and again, into depths most of us never experience. Every physical, emotional, mental and spiritual blow seems to slam this young woman further and further down into the pits of despair. Yet, Tracy shows us how to exist in the pit and climb on wings of faith, up from the very bottom.

This is one those "Good gracious, when will the sista get a break?" books! It helps us to know that storms arise quickly and come with devastating powers. Tracy has never led a charmed life. She knows the reality of struggle, challenge, questions, pain, abandonment, betrayal and rejection. She understands the severe testing of family betrayal and loss of hope. She walks us through her hopes, dreams and even fantasies of "happily ever after!" Tracy helps us to comprehend that many of our common myths are simply childhood illusions which must be addressed, faced and overcome if we want to come through the storms of life with good success.

I met Tracy over ten years ago. She became my adopted daughter. Even then, Tracy understood the need to "see" the lessons of life and to learn from them how to become her best self. Today, Tracy is my friend. For we have been through many pit experiences together. At times, she is my counselor. Some times she even has been my mother! For we are like Naomi and Ruth. We need both sets of our personality traits, our devotion to each other and our individual commitment to the required journey towards wholeness and good mental health as bodacious women of color. We walk together seeking the feast with The Bread of Life!

The Naomi and Ruth story details a relationship where loss, grief, depression, search and many tears are themes of their life storms. This is a story where Naomi changes her name to Ms. Bitter because life has been so cruel. She tries to shed herself of every responsibility, including the relationship with Ruth, her daughter-in-law. She does not want company. She doesn't feel the need to engage in social chit-chat. She simply wants to wallow in her pain. Ruth makes a covenant to move from her stance of depending upon Naomi to the foreground with leadership skills she has seen modeled in better days. She declares to Ms. Bitter, "I also know pain and suffering. I too have experienced loss and grief. Yet, I will not leave you. I will not walk away. Where you go, I will go. Where you stay, I will stay. Your people shall be my people. Your God will be my God."

God carried them both through the storm. God took them from famine to feast. God moved them through depression to community celebration. Read the Biblical Story and be encouraged. This is one of those "God of Comfort, stop by here." books. For Naomi and Ruth's story is my and Tracy's story. It can be yours too. God is just that way! For God delights in seeing us, being with us and carrying us through the eye of every storm. Buckle up. It's moving time!

With every prayer for you as you settle in for a worthy read, a powerful testimony and source of encouragement as you watch the storms in your life teach you and defeat you, I bid you Shalom, my friend, God's very best Shalom!

Rev. Dr. Linda H. Hollies, Author, ***Inner Healing for Broken Vessels and Jesus and Those Bodacious Women***

Preface

Dear Bishop Butler,

Over the past year, I've been lead to share my personal testimony with you on several occasions. I pray that my story will be a blessing to someone and God will get all the glory and praise!!

Although I'm not new to the body of Christ (I've loved the Lord since I was seven years old. Glory to God!), I've only been at Word of Faith (WOF) since February 1997. Initially, I began worshiping at Word because the young man I was dating politely insisted that we worship together. Since service at Word of Faith is early, I agreed to worship with him and then to go to my own church. As time went on and the Word came forth, the Holy Spirit moved my heart to become a part of the Word of Faith family. In the beginning, I struggled. I didn't want to leave my home church -- all my roots are there...I grew up there...I was baptized there...my family heritage is there. I asked myself over and over again if I was just doing this because of the person I was dating. Thank God for the Holy Spirit who kept working with me. One Sunday during altar call, I felt someone tap me. I turned around and no one was sitting behind me. I later shared this with my friend who echoed that the Lord was prompting me. I experienced several similar events and finally one Sunday morning in September of 1997, I found myself "suddenly" at the altar. I now know that my friend was but a vessel God used to bring me where he wanted me to be. Word of Faith is now my "church".

I have been so blessed by the many ministries at WOF. God has taken me to higher levels and deeper depths in him. I do believe that it is because of the anointing and the uncompromising "Word" that I can share my testimony with you today.

Introduction

Storms are not new to me. At an early age, I became familiar with life's storms. Born in January 1962, I am the oldest child of Leo and Betty Flaggs. My brother, Brian, whom I affectionately call "Flaggs", was born in January of 1964.

As long as I can remember, Brian and I have had a special brother/sister bond. We've always been there for each other, loved each other, cared for each other and supported each other no matter what. If we had to, we would literally move mountains for each other.

As a growing child, I'm not sure I realized how unique and rare our relationship really was. Like most siblings, we would fuss with each other almost constantly; however, if anyone else tried, I would quickly say, "That's my brother" and Brian would say, "That's my sister." Instinctively, without being prompted, we would stand up for each other.

I have grown to know that our relationship is not common. Perhaps the special bond developed because for most of our growing years, we only had each other. We are the one stable force in each other's lives that remains constant and true. No matter what storm comes our way, we stand together. You see, we experienced loss at a very early age. The first storm of our lives was when our mother died. I was three and Brian was still a baby.

My maternal grandmother – "Grandma Bowie" – then reared us until she died in 1968, four years later, yet another storm in our young lives. I still have vivid memories of "Grandma Bowie's" love and teachings. A woman of God, Grandma Bowie taught us to pray, read and recite the 23rd Psalm and sing "Yes, Jesus loves me." I believe it is because of this strong spiritual legacy that I began to know and develop a personal relationship with God at the early age of seven.

When Grandma Bowie died, we stayed with several relatives and then our Dad before my paternal grandparents – John and

Gertie – told my Dad "to go get those children and bring them with us." I'll never forget the day my Dad took us to Grandma Gertie's house to live. My Grandma cried and said, "God has finally answered my prayer."

My grandparents, who I affectionately called "Sweetie and Gramps" in my adult life, raised my brother and I with love, commitment and determination. As God fearing grandparents, they raised us to stand for what was right and true, to believe in ourselves and to know with God nothing was impossible. They taught us by example to love and dream. They constantly told us to make sure at the end of the day we had given our very best to ourselves, our family and our community.

Although my grandparents (both maternal and paternal) have been key driving forces in my upbringing, others have played vital roles as well. I have a large extended family of aunts, uncles, cousins, godparents, life long family friends, neighbors, teachers, church mothers and dads – who have all been pieces of fabric in the quilt of my life. As the African proverb says, it has truly taken a village to raise a child...Each person teaching me in their own unique way how to weather the storms of life.

Little did I know that these examples and experiences would prepare me for the biggest storm of my life.

* * * * *

It was a clear, sunny, bright fall day. No real clouds in the sky. Seemingly, a great day for a Caribbean Cruise – a day to relax and sail on the water!

After hours of enjoying the peaceful serenity of the ocean, the beaming sun and the fresh cool breeze, it was time to head back to shore.

As we turned to go inland, suddenly without warning the water became choppy, the wind's velocity increased and threatening clouds appeared. After a beautiful day at sea, a storm was developing. There had been no mention of a storm, as a matter of fact, the weather report predicted excellent weather for boating. In addition, there had been no small motor craft warnings.

"Where did this storm come from?" I wondered. Nonetheless, we must hurry if we are to reach shore before the storm, I thought. Within minutes, the sky became dark. The wind began gusting and there was intense rainfall. The visibility was so poor, I could not see the other passengers or my hands in front of me.

The waves began breaking and moving rapidly. With each wave, the small boat was lifted upward in a different direction. The captain screamed, "I can't tell which way the storm is headed. It seems to be coming from all directions." Recognizing that the storm was developing too fast for us to get ashore, the captain called the Coast Guard for help. Yet, there was no answer.

In an instant, the waves breaking over the boat seemed to be 10-12 feet high. "Dear Lord, please don't let us sink," I prayed. The wind was howling like never before. It was a roaring noise I had never heard before. It must be a hurricane!

Just at that second, I was tossed across the deck by the force of the wind and waves. Everything on the boat was flying everywhere. I frantically groped for the side railing, *but my hands were too wet to hold on.* Another wave came quickly and this time I was thrown overboard. I held on for dear life to something that appeared to be a raft. I was literally holding on by my fingernails as I was tossed and driven with every wind and wave. This seemed to go on for days, weeks and months -- each moment feeling like an eternity!

The people in the boat panicked. They were yelling and screaming not really knowing what to do. They seemed to toss me a lifeline, yet I could not reach it. All I could do was hold on. I was frightened, scared and terrified, "What on earth was happening?"

A million thoughts of what to do went through my mind as I hung there fighting for my life with every ounce of my being, yet I could not move. I kept affirming I will live and not die, I will hold on. I can't and I won't give up!

With the next twelve foot wave, I was thrown back on the boat. "Will this storm ever pass?" I asked. I was now cold and wet from the exposure. I was pale and frail. I was not fully aware of my surroundings or what was happening. Although several people rushed to assist and care for me, no one really heard my cries for help. "Lord, please hold me and bring me through this storm," I prayed.

I was bruised and scared yet I was alive. I survived the worst storm of my life…a storm that seemed to be a hurricane.

Hurricanes are some of nature's most devastating storms. They develop from a series of thunderstorms and they are often deadly. No one really knows why some storms dissipate and never develop while others become full blown hurricanes causing massive destruction.

Some storms are unexpected, sudden, intense, devastating and life changing; like the illness in my life that began in October of 1997….

Chapter One

Storm Development

October 13, 1997, I was at work feeling fine. My schedule on Mondays was always hectic and this particular Monday was no exception to the rule. It began with a mentoring meeting with one of my bosses. During our conversation he stopped and said, "Boy, you don't look good." I responded by saying, "That's funny...I feel fine. Now, last week was a different story. I felt as if I had the flu and I had to keep coaching myself to keep one foot in front of the other. I rested over the weekend and now I feel fine." Our meeting continued and ended just in time for us to make it to our next manager's meeting. However, his words stayed on my mind because he was not one to comment one way or the other on someone's appearance. At my first opportunity, I called my doctor who told me to come in later that day at 3:00 p.m. Leaving the office early was always a major challenge but this day I made sure I left in enough time to make my appointment. After close examination, my doctor insisted that I probably had "one of those viruses" going around. However, since I was known to say "I am too busy to be sick," my doctor said he was admitting me to the hospital to make sure I did what he said. "I know you will do what I say if I put you in the hospital for a few days."

To his surprise, I gave no resistance. Little did I know at this time that this would be only the beginning of a major attack on my body and spirit. Little did I know that a major storm – a hurricane – was developing in my life. A storm which would go on for days,...weeks,...and even months. The attack would be unrelenting and when the enemy couldn't take my life, the attack would then turn to my spirit – stealing my joy and shaking my faith was the goal. "But what was meant for evil by the enemy, God allowed for my good and his glory!" Little did I know I would be ***caught in the "I" of the storm.***

I left my doctor's office and drove myself to the hospital. I called my friend from the car to let him know what was going on. As I sat in my room that evening after being admitted to McLaren Hospital (Flint, Michigan), my friend came in. He insisted that I had been running too much, burning the candle at both ends. Before he left, he lead us in prayer and declared that the blood of Jesus would cover and protect me from any hurt, harm or danger.

After running several tests the next day, my doctor informed me that indeed I had a virus. In addition, all my major systems were "depleted". My potassium level was so low, it was surprising I had not had a heart attack. My key proteins and electrolytes were all off. I was also dehydrated. The treatment of antibiotics and fluids would begin immediately. My doctors were sure everything would be back to normal within a few days. I thanked and praised the Lord that he had protected me. For you see, everyday I drove 60 miles one way from my house to the office. I could have passed out driving to work or worse yet I could have fallen out at home while I was alone. "God is so good" I exclaimed, "He is protecting us when we don't even realize it."

My hospitalization at McLaren continued for weeks. I seemed to get better but then without rhyme or reason I wouldn't hold a meal on my stomach. This was unusual since I had always been relatively healthy. My doctors ran every test they could think of to help determine the root cause. Every test came back negative. It appeared that this virus had to run its course. I continued to feel better but I started losing weight and gradually became anemic. Eventually, I couldn't keep anything on my stomach. Although I believed I was healed, I couldn't help but wonder what was going on. I became anxious. What was my body trying to communicate? Had I missed some valuable warning signs? Was this my body's way of forcing me to slow down? If so, I decided to get still before the Lord and let God minister to me.

During this time, I spent most of my days listening to the Word of God on tape, praising the Lord with gospel music, studying the Scriptures and witnessing. When anyone would call me I would declare, "God is faithful and I am healed." I would say, "No weapon formed against me shall prosper."

As I laid in the hospital day after day, God would speak to me by revealing scriptures I had never read or heard before. One day I opened my Bible to read my Daily Word and my Bible opened to ***Psalm 138:8, "The Lord will make perfect that which concerns me."*** The Lord also revealed another new scriptural verse to me in my Bible study: ***Psalm 46:10, "Be still and know that I am God."*** As I look back, God was allowing me the time to prepare for the journey ahead.

November 3, 1997 began my fourth week at McLaren Hospital. Days and weeks had passed and there had been no change in my condition. My doctors were now concerned that I wasn't getting significantly better with the prescribed treatment. It was determined that on Tuesday, my doctor would take another scope that had previously been taken to see if there was any change. This would be done at 6:00 p.m. so my brother, my friend and my primary doctor could be present.

A scope of my colon was taken that evening. According to my doctors, the virus had attacked my entire digestive system and lodged itself in my colon. My entire colon was now inflamed. Medically they believed we were losing ground and emergency surgery was inevitable. Although both my doctors were very professional, it was obvious to me that they were both very concerned and alarmed. My primary doctor saw the scope and said, "Oh my God, it is like wild fire." I responded by saying, **"Don't worry, I serve an *"on time"* God. He is always on time, never late."** After everyone composed themselves, my doctors talked to my brother, my friend and me. My doctors insisted on making sure I had the best possible care. This would mean traveling three hours to The Cleveland Clinic. One of my doctors personally knows the world renowned surgeon who specializes in treating people with conditions similar to mine. This surgeon has operated on the Pope and other people of notoriety. At the time, I did not know The Cleveland Clinic was a world excellent hospital and world class benchmark for treatment. Look at God! Even in the midst of the storm, God provided the very best for his daughter. I was reminded once again that God would make perfect everything that concerned me. The care and expertise The Cleveland Clinic provided was second to none and was a vital part of saving my life.

My friend and my brother remained strong and positive in my presence. I can only imagine how they felt. I'm not sure which is more challenging going through the storm yourself or watching someone you love go through the storm. Those who watch you go through have a lot of feelings of their own. However, because they believe that they must remain strong for you often their feelings are suppressed. No one knew, at the time, that my major health challenges were just ahead of me.

On the night before we left for The Cleveland Clinic, once I was alone, I took a nice warm shower to try to relax my mind and body. A million thoughts ran through my head. I wasn't totally sure what was about to happen to me. As I stepped into the shower and the water began to run, I began crying uncontrollably. "Oh Lord, what is about to happen to me, I cried? I know I am healed! Daddy, I need you to hold me and bring me through this storm. No one but you will truly hear my cry for help. No one but you will truly know my pain. Daddy I need you to carry me through," I cried. One tear came then a river of tears began to flow. I cried until I could cry no more. Then "suddenly" as I turned the shower off, the Holy Spirit spoke to me in a still small voice, "***your life is in my hands***."

We arrived at The Cleveland Clinic (CCF) on Thursday evening, November 6, 1997. I felt very weak physically. I couldn't hold anything on my stomach and I had severe diarrhea. The staff at CCF was waiting for my arrival. Some preoperative testing was done and major emergency surgery was set for the next morning. Although I was in a lot of pain and unclear of everything that was about to happen to me, I felt confident that God would heal me.

My brother, my friend and I prayed before I went to surgery. We were all very positive. I remember being more concerned about them than myself. Watching your loved one go down that long hall to the operating room can not be fun. True to God's nature he sent an angel - a family friend who lived in the area – to sit with my brother and friend to lighten the load while I was in surgery.

Almost four hours later, the surgery was completed. Once I was awakened, my brother was amazed that I was so alert. I was surprisingly rattling off phone numbers of people to call. The surgeon spoke to me and said, "The surgery was a success! The good news is we were able to get to your colon 'just in time'. The bad news is that it was very toxic and could not be saved because it could have ruptured at any time. We had to remove your colon and replace it with a temporary ileostomy. We just made it. We had no time left." Had my colon burst, I would have died from the infection and poison in my body. Later surgeries would be required to repair, reconstruct and replace my colon. Once again, my God is always on time. God did not allow the enemy to take my life. The emergency surgery performed at the CCF on November 7, 1997, literally saved my life. Glory be to God!! I was excited and overwhelmed all at the same time. There would be several life adjustments; however, I was alive and doing well and that is all I wanted to focus on.

Everything seemed to be going fine. My diet would begin with clear liquids. Once I could tolerate solid foods, I would be discharged. The doctors initially thought I would go home in seven to ten days. That meant I would be home for Thanksgiving. What a blessing, I thought.

My care at the CCF was superb. "Dr. V." (my surgeon), his staff, the nurses, the support team -- everyone – took special care with me and treated my brother and friend like royalty. Several days passed and the storm appeared calm. I was progressing well. Then without warning, a hurricane developed.

"Thought For The Day"

The Lord will make perfect that which concerns you.
Psalm 138:8.

Suggestions:

What storms are developing in your life?

Have you experienced a "sudden storm" in the past year?

How did you feel?
(i.e., sad, scared, angry, etc.)

What or who can help support you during this time?
(i.e., songs, scriptures, books, family, friends)

Rest in knowing God will make perfect that which concerns you.

Reflections

Reflections

Chapter Two

Sudden Storm

Five days after major emergency surgery, on November 12, in the wee hours of the morning, I began to feel strange. I couldn't articulate to my nurse exactly what or how I was feeling. I simply didn't feel right. My nurse began to monitor me closely by taking my vital signs every few minutes. It seemed that my blood pressure was dropping. She contacted my doctor. When the doctor arrived, I could tell by the look on his face something serious was wrong. Everyone began scurrying around and I was sent to the intensive care unit immediately.

My family was contacted. When my brother and my family arrived, I was hooked up to several machines with what appeared to be a thousand tubes attached to me. My nieces were frightened and my sister-in-law began crying. I remember reassuring my sister-in-law. "Oh no Marian, don't cry. I am going to be fine. I'm going to lick this. God is faithful." I would later learn that it was discovered that a blood clot had developed and it was moving toward my lungs and heart. My sister-in-law was crying because she knew had it reached my lungs or heart, it would have killed me. The blood clot was believed to have formed because of an earlier pick line that was put in because I have small veins. The protection of God and the power of prayer is so awesome. God never allowed me to be consciously aware of all the life threatening events that were taking place. I actually never knew when I was going through this how grave my medical condition was. I have lived the song "Someone Prayed For Me." My family, my friend, my extended family, friends, colleagues, people on the CCF staff and people I didn't even know prayed for me.

Sometimes life's events are such that you are not able to read your Bible or pray for yourself. That is why it is so important to meditate on the Word of God daily and put it in your heart while you can. The scripture which says, out of the mouth comes the issues of the heart, speaks to the Word of God being placed in your heart. If the Word is already in your heart, it will come forth and no weapon formed against you shall prosper (Isaiah 54:17). If the Word is not in your heart already, it can not come forth. We can not afford the luxury of being lax. One day your very life could depend upon the Word of God that resides in your heart.

I returned to a regular room several days later. My physical body was in a life threatening crisis. I was now on a lot of strong medications to dissolve the blood clot and to save my life. Several of the medicines had major side effects. In addition, it seemed that my body began producing anti-bodies because of the crisis it was in. When your body produces antibodies it is fighting against itself to rid the body of anything foreign. While this is happening, it is easy for the body to become overwhelmed and actually defeat its intended purpose and die.

My friend was an angel. Every Friday evening, no matter the weather, no matter where I was or my condition, he was at my side speaking the Word and believing God for my complete healing. I can only imagine what he must have felt. His strength and spiritual leadership was paramount. He literally refused to let me die. It is so critical to surround yourself with people who will stand in faith, no matter what. People of wavering faith can cost you your life.

Several weeks passed and I was still critically ill. No one seemed to know specifically why. Thanksgiving 1997 came and went. I was so sick I was literally in a fog. I remember being very frustrated, but never once did I doubt I was healed.

God sent several angels in human form to encourage me. "Belinda" was a visiting nurse from the University of Chicago, who briefly cared for me. One night before she returned to Chicago, she came to my room. She said she was my angel and she insisted everything would be alright. "The spirit of the Lord is all on you!" I asked when I would see her again? She replied, "We may not see each other until we get to the other side. But you're going to be alright." I became adamant and replied, "No I want to see you again before then! I want to see you when I am healed."

Another angel was Daisybelle. Daisybelle is a very dear sister/girlfriend who lived in the local area. She and her husband, Nelson, would come and hold my hand while reminding me that God would never leave me. Daisybelle whispered the words of the Psalmist - David in my ear. She would begin passages of scriptures and asked me to complete the verse. This was so powerful because several times I was in and out of consciousness. Yet, Daisybelle helped me speak the Word on my situation. You see the Word gives life. The Word of God heals and darkness can not exist when the Word shines the light of truth on it. The Word is truth. No matter what the natural facts say, The Word of God is the truth. Daisybelle had me speak the truth to my situation even when the circumstances said differently. Daisybelle had me speaking Scriptural verses even though I wasn't fully conscious. Glory to God! When you are fighting for your life, you must have people around you that will speak the Word of God only! Hallelujah!

Daisybelle also knew I loved teddy bears so she brought me a soft pink bear to hold. God is so faithful. Even in the midst of the storm, God is faithful!!!

In addition, several local ministers would visit regularly and pray with me no matter what my condition was. One particular visit remains vivid in my mind. One of the ministers was praying for me and he said, "Lord, your servant Tracy has been so faithful whether she stays or goes on to be with you, it is all good." Although I was critically ill, I remember thinking and saying to myself "I have no idea what he is talking about. I am not going anywhere. I did not come here to die. I will live! I will not die." Hallelujah!

Once again, speaking the Word – God's word is the key. Speaking the truth on your situation is what gives life. Speaking the Word in faith is what will cause your condition to change! Glory to God! When you are in a crisis – especially a life threatening crisis – **you can not afford to just say anything and you can't allow others to just say anything.** ***You must speak the Word of God only!***

As I reflect, it is so important for those who are caregivers or serve in hospital or nursing home ministries to be careful when speaking to patients. You must remain prayerful and positive at all times. Although it may appear that the person can't hear you or can't respond, most of the time they can. Words have power. You must speak the Word of God only. Speaking the Word – the truth – gives life and can cause what looks like a bleak situation to turn around. Being prayerful and speaking what God says about the situation instead of speaking what the circumstances say is the key.

Six weeks later in December, I returned to the operating room for a second time and two days later for a third time for major emergency surgeries before I slowly began to recover. To this day, medically no one can explain why I had so many complications. However, on the other hand, all my doctors agree, "I am a walking miracle!" I know, God supernaturally removed the blood clot! God brought me through all three surgeries when medically I didn't have a chance. Only God could have done it! I am truly a miracle! To God be all the glory, honor and praise!

"Thought For the Day"

"Whose report will you believe?"
I will believe the report of the Lord."

Suggestions:

If you are going through a storm in your life,
Write down what the natural facts say
Then search the scriptures for what God
has to say about your circumstances.
Decide to focus on what God says
And not man.

Reflections

Reflections

Chapter Three

The Silent Storm

Everyone was elated that I would be home for Christmas. Both my brother and friend believed if they could just get me home my recovery would be faster and our lives would return to normal. Plans were made to make Christmas extra special for me. Little did we know, the healing process was only beginning; consequently, for me Christmas 1997 is only a blur.

I was so weak when I came home I could hardly stand up. My physical body had gone through so many traumatic events and my outward appearance reflected the health challenges I endured. I had lost so much weight, I looked like a ghost and several people didn't recognize me. My face was covered with what looked like a million spots. There was literally no skin free of bumps. This was extremely significant because I had always had flawless skin. My brother screamed when he first saw me. In addition, I was gradually being weaned off large doses of medicine and for the first time in my life, my blood pressure was sky high.

As long as I can remember, I've had a bubbling "sunshine" personality. God has given me a joy for life that is indescribable. However, at this time, I wanted to smile yet I couldn't. I desperately wanted to express the joy that was still deep down in my soul but I was so weak, I couldn't. A few people honestly admitted they could not stand to see me in this state. I had always been a strong, independent, vibrant person and seeing me like this was too much for them to handle. It was then I realized the enemy couldn't take my life so now the attack was on my spirit. The enemy was now after my joy and my faith.

There were many days, nights and weeks that I cried uncontrollably. What was happening to me? My world had turned upside down in a matter of months. I felt frightened, sad and lonely. "Lord, hold me and bring me through this storm," I prayed. Although I struggled a lot, never once did I think I wasn't going to make it. As a matter of fact, I refused to die. "I may be down but I will not die. I'll rise again", I said. I was determined not to give in or give up. My 36th birthday came and went in January of 1998 and I kept confessing the Word. I kept declaring that human hands may fail me, but God said he would never leave me nor forsake me and God cannot lie!

True to his word, God never left me. As a matter of fact, many days he carried me. On those days that I felt weak and unsure of what lay ahead, God would send an angel to uplift me. A phone call, an unexpected visitor or a package would arrive which brightened my day and encouraged me to stand strong.

One particular day, I returned from my doctor's appointment to find a Federal Express package on my porch. Upon opening the envelope, I discovered my boss and mentor had sent me a CD by Donnie McClurkin. Only God could have done such a thing. The song "Stand" on the CD ministered to my entire being.

> "Tell me what do you do, when you've done all you can,
> And it seems like you can't make it through?
> Child you just stand….
> Don't you dare give up
> Through the storm, through the rain,
> Through the hurt,
> Through the pain.
> Don't you bow and don't you bend.
> Don't give up, no don't give in
> Hold on, just be strong.
> God will step in and it won't be long…
> After you've done all you can
> You just stand"

I would play "Stand" over and over again. Like David, I would sing, shout and dance before the Lord.

I have also been blessed with doctors that love the Lord and truly care about me as a person. They were invaluable at this time.

They assured me that I would get through these life changing events. "The journey will be long but you will get through it," they all said.

It was during this time that I realized unequivocally that I could not get through these traumatic events on my own strength. I knew I had to draw even closer to God and reach out to the body of Christ for encouragement. I knew without a doubt that I was totally and solely dependent upon God to get me through in every area of my life: physically, spiritually, emotionally, financially and socially.

This was significant for me. For you see, although I have been committed to the Lord since I was seven, I have always been a very passionate, intense, logical thinking and organized person; two plus two must equal four. No other answer is possible. To really sit still and let go completely to God and not try to figure out every single detail was very challenging. My daily prayer was, "Lord I yield my will to your perfect will for every area of my life. Your plan for my life is good and prosperous." (Jeremiah 29:11) I also decided not to focus on myself. Instead, my desire was to be a blessing to whomever I could. There is something about "giving" that heals. When you give, God gives so much more to you. The spiritual law of giving says give and it will be given to you. In good measure, pressed down, shaken together and running over. When you totally surrender your will to God's divine plan for your life, God reveals his true nature. I began soaking up God's Word. Not only did I study the Word and meditate on it, I began to share it with others like never before. As I began to share, God put people in my path that were hurting and needed encouragement. As I encouraged, I became encouraged.

One day I was sifting through some old notes and I ran across the phone number of the Word Cell Section Leader in my area, "Sister DD." I called her and to my surprise she knew exactly who I was. Apparently she had been calling me for months but was never able to reach me. I explained in general terms why we had not connected. She praised the Lord that I had called and invited me to the next meeting. Look at God again! "Sister DD" is such a beautiful example of how God never gives up on us.

"Sister DD" called me regularly for weeks and months with no response from me. At the time, she didn't know I was in the hospital or that I was experiencing serious health challenges. She never knew what I was going through. She had no way of knowing that I was fighting for my life. Instead, she just kept following the Holy Spirit. She stood in faith not knowing my specific situation. She just kept following God and she never stopped calling me. She never gave up. Finally, one day, I was able to return her calls. Hallelujah! God is so faithful! When I think of "Sister DD" and her love and persistence, I am reminded of a message I heard by Dr. Forbes "What to do with the Pressure." "Don't quit, don't faint and don't give in. You never know what's going on the other side of the phone receiver...We don't know what God is doing on the other side...That's why we call God - "Jehovah, Off The Hook"– the phone receiver is always on its way off the hook. God can always turn it around. He is one step...one ring away from answering your call! Don't give up...Don't give in..." God never allowed "Sister DD" to give up on me! Praise God.

I love Word Cell at Word of Faith (WOF). Word Cell Ministries is an extension of the church's outreach ministry where attendees meet in small groups in each other's homes once a week to worship, praise God, pray, study the Word, uplift and encourage each other. Since Word of Faith is a large church, the Word Cell Ministry is a way of keeping the church small and personal. Word Cell has been a tremendous blessing to me. Everyone has reached out and touched my life in such a special way. I praise God for giving Bishop Keith A. Butler the vision of Word Cell Ministries! It really works!!

I began attending Thursday night worship service regularly. Since I wasn't working, I didn't allow anything to stop me from being in the service. Not feeling well was not an acceptable reason to miss as far as I was concerned.

As I began to reach out, I was blessed as well. My appetite returned and I began to eat. By Resurrection Sunday 1998 (known to some as Easter Sunday), I had gained most of my weight back. My strength and stamina were slowly returning.

By May of 1998, I had made tremendous progress. I was walking several miles a day, my blood pressure was finally normal, my major systems, proteins, and electrolytes were back on track and I was off all medication! My doctors were amazed. Other people would comment that they knew God was real when they saw me because no one but God could do such a thing!! I was reminded of God's Word, "Be still and know that I am God."

I received a call from Cleveland Clinic (CCF) verifying my June 26 follow-up appointment. At this time my surgeon would evaluate how well I was healing and determine if future surgeries could be done. Future surgeries would be necessary if I wanted to fully return to a normal life style.

When I received the call, I initially panicked. "I'm just now beginning to feel like myself again. My strength and stamina have finally returned. I plan to go back to work soon. My life is just getting back to normal and you want me to go through another two surgeries. No thank you," I thought.

My mind continued to race a million miles a minute. I thought about all the days I cried out to the Lord to hold me and to bring me through the storm. I thought about the days and weeks that went by that I saw no sun. I literally saw no one except the home care nurse that came to care for me. I thought about the struggle to get my life back. A struggle that very few people not even those closest to me really understood. My physical and emotional being had endured so much. "Not now," I thought. "Maybe next year, but not now." I wish I could say I laughed at the enemy for bombarding me with all these distracting thoughts but I didn't. I was scared.

I called my friend who echoed that he didn't know that if it were him, he would have the additional surgeries either. "All that you've been through. I don't know if I would have anymore surgeries", he said.

My friend and my family had watched me fight for my life and fight to get back on my feet. Each one was excellent support. I had the best care. There was stress and strain on everyone. We were all stretched to the limit for different reasons. Candidly speaking, no one was excited about going through this process again – Especially Me!

It was not until I spoke to my doctors a few days later that I began to relax and know that God was in control. My doctors finally shared with me in graphic detail how grave my medical condition had been when I had the surgery in November 1997. "No one said this to you at the time but we were only counting on prayer to pull you through. Medically, you didn't have a chance. You are so much stronger now. Your body is built up to its normal self. All your major systems are within normal range. There are certain risks with having any surgery. The longer you wait the higher the risk. Unless there is a good reason why you cannot have the surgery in August, you must complete the process. Going back to work is not an acceptable reason," they both said. I praised God for my doctors. They allowed the Holy Spirit to use them as the vessels that I needed to move forward. I was reminded to be still and know that I am God's. I was reminded that God is faithful and he promised to make perfect everything that concerns me. I was reminded of all God's miracles in my life – not just with this health challenge but all throughout my life, God's been good to me! No matter what the circumstance, he has never left nor forsaken me. As I began to think on and rest in the presence of God's awesomeness, I got a peace in my spirit to continue on.

Thought For The Day

"No test, no testimony."
Said to me by Precious Lee on December of 1997.

Suggestions:

What silent storm are you facing?
Make a list of how you feel.
Cry if you must.
Then speak to God and let Him know all about it.
(He already knows.)

Let go and let God handle it for you.
Cast your cares on Him for he cares for you.

Reflections

Reflections

Chapter Four

Disturbance on the Horizon

It was at this time that I began to prepare myself for the upcoming surgeries. I was now determined to press ahead. I knew I had to be physically and emotionally strong to endure several additional major surgeries. I knew that the enemy would try to distract me if given an opportunity. As I moved forward, I was reminded that God is able to do exceedingly, abundantly, above all you can think of or imagine...(Ephesians 3:20)

Once again the ministries at Word of Faith (WOF) were invaluable. I called the church to speak to someone on the ministerial staff. I did not want to proceed without someone at my church knowing what I was facing. I didn't ask for anyone specifically. I just needed to talk to someone. I was scheduled with Pastor "T".

God is so good! Little did I know God would use Pastor "T" to minister to me and tailor our conversation to speak to my every concern. At our first meeting, I learned that Pastor "T" came to Detroit from the church in California that one of my Aunts attends. "Pastor and Mrs. T" personally knew my Aunt Ella and first cousins. Praise God!! I had no way of knowing this because I wasn't a member at WOF when Pastor "T" joined the staff. Look at God!! Since I'm such a private person and new to the church, God knew I would feel more comfortable sharing the traumatic life changing events with someone who had some history with my family.

Before we began talking, Pastor "T" asked God for his guidance and wisdom in our meeting. After prayer, I shared with Pastor "T" in general detail the events of the last eight months. While I was talking, Pastor "T" was taking notes as he was lead by the Spirit. After directing me to scriptures and prompting me to look at the root cause of my situation, he shared his notes with me. At this time, I knew the Holy Spirit was leading him because there was no way he could have known my fears about the upcoming surgeries, the changes in my personal appearance or my job, because I had not shared them with him! Look at God. God anointed Pastor "T" to minister to my every concern. I could feel the Spirit of the Lord flowing in Pastor "T"'s office that afternoon! His prescription was to identify all the healing scriptures, read and say them at least three times daily and to follow-up with him before my surgery in August.

I did exactly what he said. The following Sunday I got tapes and books on healing from the WOF bookstore. I looked up scriptures on healing. I wrote the Word on sheets of paper and placed them everywhere in my home so I could affirm my healing continuously. I declared that there would be no complication before, during or after the surgery.

My appointment at Cleveland Clinic on June 26 went exceptionally well. I met with my surgeon and several of his staff members. Dr. "V" (my surgeon) was amazed at my progress. After close examination, it was determined that I was ready for the next surgery which was confirmed for August 11, 1998. I was told that the surgery would take approximately four hours and my hospital stay would be seven to ten days. It wasn't clear on how much time would be needed for me to get back on my feet, however, the last surgery was tentatively scheduled for November 17, 1998.

Plans were made for my care at the hospital, as well as, when I returned home after surgery. I wanted to make sure someone was with me during my hospitalization and at least four weeks after surgery. If at all possible, I wanted to stay at my own home and heal. True to God's word, he supplied all my needs. Several friends asked to assist my brother and my friend in taking care of me.

I met with Pastor "T" two weeks before my surgery. He confirmed what God had already spoken to me. "This time has been a time of preparation. Something good is about to happen. There will be no complication in surgery. As a matter of fact, the surgery will be simple. You will be better than before. Keep your eyes on God. Follow the way of peace and do not deviate", he said.

True to the enemies nature, there were a lot of opportunities to lose heart, to quit and to get distracted as the date of my fourth major surgery drew near. You see, as victory approaches the enemy will work overtime to get you to lose sight of the blessing that God has already promised. No matter what comes your way, you can't give in, you can't give up. You must press ahead (Philippians 3:13-14)!

One such event that remains fresh in my mind is when my seven year old niece started crying uncontrollably as we drove home from getting ice cream at Dairy Queen. Ariel knew I would be leaving soon for another surgery at Cleveland Clinic (CCF). "Auntie, are you going to be like you were before, will you look like you looked before? Auntie, are you going to be alright?" she asked. It took all the strength I had to hold back my own tears and to confidently reassure Ariel that all was well! I responded by saying, "Cupcake, I know you're afraid. I know you remember how Auntie was before but look at Auntie now! How does Auntie look now?" "You look great," she said. "Well God brought Auntie through before and God will do it again. You just pray and ask God to keep your Auntie and he will," I reassured her. As we continued to drive and as I held her hand, it was at that very moment I realized how much everyone had been emotionally affected by my health challenges and my near death experiences in the fall of 1997. I was now more determined that God would do exceedingly abundantly more than I could ever ask or imagine. All I had to do was stand on God's Word and not deviate!!

Indeed the surgery was a success! There were no problems in surgery or in post operative recovery. The doctors were pleased with my progress. I was expected to be in the hospital seven to ten days. I was released in five!! Look at God, I just had my fourth major surgery in less than a year and I was doing well. No one but God could do such a thing.

It is amazing what God has allowed the medical community to accomplish. In a matter of four hours, reconstruction of my colon was completed. A pelvic pouch was made that replaced my colon and a temporary site was made to allow my body to heal before the last surgery. The last surgery would entail closure of the temporary site and connection of the pouch for a normal lifestyle.

I was released from the hospital on Sunday, August 16, 1998. Everyone was excited. My doctors, the staff at Cleveland Clinic, my family and my friend. There was so much joy in the air. Unspeakable joy!!!! No one verbalized it, but, everyone was really relieved that the surgery was successful, my hospital stay was short and I was now going home to heal.

A funny thing happened on the way home. My brother, sister-in-law and nieces stopped at the rest area while I was asleep. At the time, I did not need to use the facilities. However, approximately half hour later, I woke up with a tremendous urge to go to the bathroom. I told my brother who was driving and he informed me that we had just passed the rest area and the next one was several miles away. What could we do? I knew I could not wait. After driving another few miles, I asked him to pull over. He was reluctant, however, I insisted. I could not wait any longer. I had to pee! "Flaggs" (my brother) did pull over and I barely made it. After major surgery, you don't have complete control over your bladder. When your body signals you to pee…you have to pee right away! I pulled up my dress and squatted in the tall grass along the side of the road while my youngest niece, Alyxis yelled "Auntie Tracy is peeing on the grass!" Everyone laughed including me. "What a relief!"

My four year old niece was a perfect example of the excitement in the air. Alyxis jumped on my bed once we arrived home and exclaimed "Auntie, you're home. You did it! We did it! Uncle Nate, my Daddy, my Mommy, Ariel and me, we did it! You're home!" I responded with a smile. "Yes Auntie's home. Remember God promised Auntie would be alright and God did it…Auntie's home!"

The insight of children constantly amazes me. No one made a big fuss about this major victory. As a matter of fact, we all acted as if this accomplishment was normal. Somehow, Alyxis knew without being told that this success – this victory-- was something to celebrate. Look at God! Even Alyxis knew that it was time for praise and celebration for what God had done. My entire family including the little ones were a witness to the miracles of the Lord!!

I was equally elated about being home. However, I must admit I was exhausted from the drive home and all the excitement. I just wanted to climb into my own bed and go to sleep. Sweet rest was all I desired that beautiful Sunday summer evening.

The first week I was home was so special. My sister/girlfriends from Lansing, Michigan came to care for me. Ann, Vernell and Maxine were God's special angels sent to remind me again that God will supply all your needs. They took care of whatever I needed large or small. They wouldn't let me do anything. They all gave of themselves unselfishly. For you see, it takes a special kind of person to take care of others in their time of need. Especially a person who is accustomed to doing everything for herself. I am truly grateful for the gift of true friendship.

The second night I was home in the wee hours of the morning, I was awakened with an overwhelming sense of praise. I began singing and thanking the Lord for all he had done. I thanked him for showing himself true over and over and over again. I was so moved by the Spirit of the Lord I was oblivious to my surroundings. My praise and worship continued for hours. I was so caught up in the presence of the Lord, I totally forgot Ann was in the next room. It is so hard to put into words what I experienced that night. Yet, I know I felt the presence of the Lord like never before! God let me know that the closer walk with him that I asked for years ago, I now had. I had finally gotten still and let God show himself to me. I was finally in position to receive all God had in store for me. That night, I knew my life would never be the same again.

The next morning, Ann told me that she knew the presence of the Lord was in my home. She said she was awakened by my praise the night before so she began communing with God as well. She said she felt peace and joy like never before. She said she knew the Holy Spirit had been in this place! Praise God! Not only had my life been changed by living the miracles of the Lord, my family and friends have also seen in living color the awesomeness of God. Hallelujah!

"Thought For the Day"

"I Win"

"The Joy of the Lord is my strength"

Suggestions:

List five examples of
major victories in your life.

Daily make a mental list of at least
ten things for which you are grateful.

Reflections

Reflections

Chapter Five

Storm Surge

As the week passed, I was on a spiritual and emotional high. My spirit was so excited and bubbling with joy. I was basking in the glow of the Lord. I also continued to feel really good physically. It was amazing how well I was doing. Little did I know storm clouds were rising and strong winds were beginning to blow. I could not have imagined that the hurricane was not over. The enemy would try again and again and again to steal my joy and break my spirit. The attack this time would intensify physically, spiritually, emotionally and financially. The attack would not be fair. It never is. Every fear I ever had would be revealed. This attack would test the very core of my being…the very essence of who I am. The goal would be to get me to quit…to lose heart…to give up. The attack was not personal. It never is. The enemy wants to get you to quit so the vision that God has for you will not come to pass. The enemy wants to get you to block or stop your own blessing.

This attack would continue for weeks and months. At the end, however, once again God would prove himself faithful. I would stand, resist the enemy and in the end victory would be mine. Above all, God would get all the glory and praise!! Indeed, no one but a mighty God could have brought me through.

The storm clouds began rising on August 21, 1998, which was eleven days after my fourth major surgery. The temporary ileostomy site began leaking on my clothes. My sister/girlfriend, Vernell who is a registered nurse helped me get cleaned up and changed. What happened? Neither one of us knew. Nevertheless, all was well now, or so we thought.

The next day once again the temporary site began leaking while I was resting. I was awakened to find all my clothes and bedding wet. What was happening? I got up to go to the bathroom and I could hardly move. I felt very weak. I called to Vernell and Maxine who were downstairs to come help me. What was wrong?? We didn't know. Nothing like this had ever happened before. Suddenly, I felt a sense of sadness come over me and I began crying uncontrollably. Until that point, I had been the model patient. Whatever came my way, I handled by praying my way through. However, for some reason, at that very moment, I felt helpless.

Vernell and Maxine were able to get everything under control. The leaking continued unpredictably for several days. No one seemed to know why. In addition, I continued to feel weak and it became a challenge to move around.

My first doctor's appointment was scheduled for August 26, 1998 which was two weeks after surgery. By this time my skin was so irritated from the leaking I was in pain and I still felt very weak. I later learned that the position of the temporary site was close to multiple nerves. The leaking could be minimized but the problem could not be solved until the last surgery. This would mean I would have to manage some level of pain for the next several months since when the temporary ileostomy would function and leak it would burn my skin causing it to be raw. The skin immediately surrounding the temporary site was affected the most. I was literally in agony.

In addition, while my body was healing and adjusting, I would lose over forty (40) pounds. I would go from a size eight (8) to barely a size two (2). My blood pressure would drop significantly causing me to have black out spells. Standing, walking and moving around in my own home would be very difficult. Eating was hard as well. I could eat, however within a few hours I would vomit. Since keeping my food down was a problem, I began to lose my appetite. My food wasn't digesting. Those who cared for me, my brother, my friend, life long family friends: Mrs. "H" and Mrs. "B", tried everything, yet, nothing seemed to work. Consequently, eating was not fun. I simply ate what I could because I had to.

Within a matter of three weeks after surgery, I was no longer able to care for myself. I couldn't drive. I couldn't cook. I could barley walk around without assistance and taking care of my basic needs was a major challenge.

It is amazing the simple things in life we take for granted. Often we go about our day never really appreciating the little things that we are able to accomplish until we suddenly are unable to do them. I was unable to take a bath. I could not stand up and dry myself off or brush my teeth! I had to sit constantly and I needed help. Getting to my bed to put on my clothes from the bathroom was difficult. It took several hours every morning to get my day started and by noon I was exhausted.

By September 8, 1998, four weeks after my fourth major surgery, it was clear that I could no longer stay at my own home. I would need to have someone care for me. Unfortunately, as much as my brother and my friend wanted to take care of me, they just couldn't. The care I required was more than they could provide. It was very difficult for everyone to admit but there was no way they could care for me and continued to also take care of their normal responsibilities.

Being totally dependent on someone especially for my basic needs was always a major fear of mine. Ever since my own Mom died 33 years ago, I always had fear of needing to depend on someone and no one being there to care for me. This is why I had built my life in such a way that I thought this would not happen. The thought of being totally dependent on someone was unbearable. I believe this is why I have been a driven person most of my life. Security is what I sought. I had unknowingly faced the fear of loss and abandonment before but never really conquered it. Praise be to God that he never gives up on us. I am so thankful that God does not cut us off when we make mistakes. He is always there with loving arms challenging us to grow and fulfill the divine purpose he has for us.

Life's journey is a faith walk. The scriptures tell us to trust in God with all our heart, lean not on our own understanding; in all our ways acknowledges him and he shall direct our path.(Proverb 3:5) God wants us...he requires us to walk by faith. Being totally dependent on God Almighty is a good thing. God said he would never leave me nor forsake me. God said he would supply my every need. God is not a man, he can not lie. My every need was already met. All I had to do was trust, believe and receive.

"Thought For the Day"

"Trust in the Lord with all your heart..."

Proverb 3:5

Suggestions:

What fears do you have?
What is the root of the fear?
It is now time to face your fear
and surrender it to God

God will supply your every need

Just let go and become
totally dependent on him.

The key is trusting God.

Reflections

Reflections

Chapter Six

Intense, Prevailing Winds and Rainfall

Facing my fear of being dependent was different this time. I was now in a place where I could finally face my fear and let it go. Actually, there was no need to be afraid because ***Jehovah Jireh*** would provide my every need and desire.

True to his word, God supplied all my needs. As I mentioned earlier, I have a large extended family who have been a major part of my life. Hope Smith, my Godmother from birth, insisted that I stay with her. She wanted to love and care for me during this time. Praise God! Aunt Hope is retired and her home is full of love and laugher. She also loves to cook.

Staying with Aunt Hope would require me to leave my home and move to Detroit, which is 50 miles away, until my last surgery in November. My brother and my friend were relieved to know that I would be in good hands. I moved in with her in September of 1998. Aunt Hope and her entire family: Daddy Yates, Kelly, Shawn, John and Eric cared for me in such a special way. They literally spoiled me.

There were so many blessings during this time. Aunt Hope, Aunt Sylvia, Von, Mrs. Henry, Mrs. Braddock, Mae Joyce, Denise Adams, Denise Marshall, Pat Churn, Ruth, Allie Paige, Word Cell, the Dixson's, Mom Allen, Aunt Mil, Aunt Ann, Brenda and so many others were invaluable. Words can not express how awesome God is. He always provides just what you need and then some. He is a God of more than enough. If you'll only trust him, stand on his Word, let go and let him handle what ever the situation is; he will show out on your behalf every time. Hallelujah!

I returned to church on September 13, 1998 for the first time since my fourth surgery in August. I was excited to be in the house of the Lord, however, I was very frail and fragile. I had lost a lot of weight and I was pale. I walked very gingerly and I was unable to stand for a long period of time. Nonetheless, I was glad to be in the service one more time!

There is power in the fellowship of the saints. You see, the scriptures tell us where two or more are gathered in his name, God will be in the midst. The Word of God also says if you ask anything in my name, believe in your heart and do not doubt whatever you ask shall be yours. Standing on the Word of God is choosing to believe what God says about your situation and not what the natural facts say. The medical facts said I could hardly walk or stand, but the Word of God says when I am weak on the outside, I am made strong through Christ who strengthens me. The Word of God says the Joy of the Lord is my strength and by his stripes I <u>was</u> healed. No matter what the facts say, God's Word is true. All you have to do is trust, believe and keep speaking the word of truth until what you are believing is physically manifested.

Although I was unable to attend Word Cell on Tuesdays, Word Cell works. Everyone continued to pray for me. At least twice a week, someone would faithfully call me and encourage me. Word Cell prayed and stood in agreement with me for my complete healing. I received cards, flowers, visits and lots of love from everyone. Sister "A" was an extraordinary blessing. She was actually my Word Cell coach! She kept affirming that in the name of Jesus, I was healed! I can't thank God enough for blessing me with such a wonderful Word Cell. Each person has blessed my life in a special way.

I returned to the Cleveland Clinic on September 28, for my eight week follow-up visit. I was scheduled to take several tests that would show my internal healing progress. I was seen by several nurses and doctors before I met with my surgeon. No one seemed to be surprised or alarmed at all the weight I had lost or my physical condition.

I saw "Dr. V", my surgeon, right before noon that day. He had read the results of all the tests and was pleased. He completed several more exams and exclaimed "You are healing to perfection." He also looked at the temporary site and commented that due to its location and size, he could see why I was experiencing so much pain and discomfort. I also explained the difficulty I was having eating. Dr. "V" shared with me that all my symptoms were normal. It was simply the body's healing process. "Don't concern yourself, everything will be fixed with your last surgery in November. Just focus on November. Your nightmares will be over. You are healing to perfection," he reassured me.

I was pleased to know I was doing so well, however, I must admit I was surprised that no one was concerned that I had lost so much weight. In addition, I wasn't sure how my body could endure another surgery when I was so small. I had no reserve, I thought.

I shared my thoughts with "Dr. B", my primary physician, on my next visit. "Dr. B" immediately corrected me and informed me she had received the report from Cleveland Clinic. No one was concerned with my weight loss because God had given me a reserve. My proteins, electrolytes and blood counts were the strongest they had ever been. They were all on the high side of the normal range, "We are not worried because we know you will be fine. You have made it through when the odds were against you medically. God has given you all you need. There is no reason for you to be concerned. God is doing his part, I am doing my part and I need you to do your part. You must prepare for your last surgery. You cannot let anything stand in the way of you receiving God's complete miracle for you!"

God is so amazing! Look at God showing himself again! When I was at my weakest on the outside, on the inside I was the strongest. Hallelujah!!

Paul put it like this in 2 Corinthians 4:16-18a - Therefore we do not lose heart though outwardly we are wasting away, yet inwardly we are being renewed day by day…so we fix our eyes not on what is seen, but what is unseen for what is seen is temporary; but the things which are not seen are eternal. In 2 Corinthians 12:9, the Word says, "My grace is sufficient for you, for my power is made perfect in weakness." Glory to God!!

God started a new work in me – from the inside…out. My health challenge was but an outward sign of the inward process. Hallelujah!!!

"Thought For The Day"

God is able to do abundantly, exceedingly more than I could ever ask or imagine.

God's power is made perfect in our weakness.

Suggestions:

What experiences have caused you great pain and distress?

What life challenges have left you feeling powerless?

Talk about your situation and your feelings with someone you trust.

Surround yourself with those who can love you through the challenge.

Know that God won't allow you to bear more than you can.

Reflections

Reflections

Chapter Seven

The "I" of the Storm

It was at this time that I began to prepare for my fifth and last surgery! I had twenty seven (27) days to go! Twenty seven (27) days before complete victory would be mine! A part of me was extremely excited, however, I must admit a part of me was overwhelmed. You see by this time, I was experiencing a lot of pain. My body was healing, however, because of the position of the temporary site, I was in excruciating pain almost constantly.

My home nurse, Kathy was a gem. She kept coaching me and assuring me that all was well! On her visits twice a week, she would always ask, "How many days until surgery?" I would reply, "You mean how many days until my victory day!"

We sing a song at Word of Faith entitled, "We Win." That song became my theme song. I would play it once in the morning and before I went to bed. I also kept a daily calendar and everyday I would count the days left until my victory day. November 17, 1998 was the day I would win! God would show out on my behalf and victory would be mine. Hallelujah!!

Moving forward, preparing for my victory was not easy. The enemy tried everything – I mean everything – to get me distracted, to get me to quit. He tried physically, financially and emotionally to get me to lose heart. Nonetheless, I would not be moved nor shaken. When I felt weak or discouraged, God would send someone to minister and encourage me to press ahead.

One particular day, I was crying uncontrollably. I was in so much pain, it was almost unbearable. In addition, my friend and I had a serious disagreement. I would later learn that during my health challenge, he was under attack as well. Like Peter, in Matthew 14:22-32, he was moving closer toward the Lord and in one split second he got distracted. He panicked and was afraid. Now the enemy was trying to sift him like wheat and destroy him. As much as I wanted to "fix" whatever the problem was; I couldn't. I had to stay focused. All I could do is pray and trust that the Word in him would come forth. I had to trust that he would resist the enemy and he would flee.

I cried out to the Lord and said, "Daddy, I know we used to sing a song in church that you won't put more on me than I can bear. Daddy, show it to me in the Word so I can stand on your promise." I asked and God revealed it to me!! Glory to God. In I Corinthians 10:12, Paul says, God has promised that he will not allow you to be tempted beyond what you can bear. When you are tempted, God will provide a way for you to stand up under the temptation or pressure. Hallelujah!! This scripture gave me the strength I needed to continue to stand although the hurricane was raging around me.

I began to feel a peace deep down in my soul. I began to praise and thank God for my victory in advance. I began to know that the blessings God had for me on the other side of this mountain were awesome. My blessings had to be beyond my imagination because Satan was trying too hard to get me to block my own blessings.

I met with Pastor "T" on Tuesday, November 3, 1998, which was fourteen (14) days before my last surgery. Pastor "T" confirmed what God had revealed to me in my study and daily prayer. "Get ready for your harvest. God is going to bless you beyond what you could ever ask or think. Just continue to praise him. God has told me that you are already praising him. Continue to get your praise on. Perfect your praise. There is victory in your praise. Get ready. It is your harvest time! Your blessings are coming!" Look at God again. He is so faithful! Truly my blessings have come and are still coming! My blessings are overtaking me! (Deuteronomy 28:1-14) There are new beginnings and blessings in every area of my life! Glory to God!

My fifth and last surgery was completed November 17, 1998. Indeed, it was a blessing. The temporary site was closed, my reconstructed colon and my digestive system were now back to normal. God showed up and he showed out!! Dr. "V" said, "The surgery was the simplest surgery he had performed." There was no scar tissue! The surgery was short and simple. Glory to God! The Cleveland Clinic staff was amazed! God not only saved my life, he healed me, made me whole and performed a medical phenomenon.

Today, I walk in divine health and wholeness. If you did not know my testimony, you would never think I had ever been sick a day in may life. Hallelujah!!

God promised through prophesies by Pastor "T" that I would be better than before and his promises are coming to pass. Job puts it like this, when I have been tried I will come forth like pure gold. (Job 23:10)

I was caught in the "I" of the storm for over 16 months. The hurricane seemed to go on endlessly. Everything around me was tossed upside down. Life as I knew it was not the same. Every area of my life and every relationship was affected. The storm went on for weeks and months. There were days when I thought the hurricane would never end. Nonetheless, in the midst of the storm, I was in the center. When you are in the center of a storm, you are safe! The center is my faith in God and my faith in his miracle working power.

I knew that God would make me whole. I knew all I would have to do is stand on his promises. When you stand in faith on God's promises, you release the power of God to perform mira cles in your life. The Word says have faith in God and do not doubt in your heart but believe and whatever you ask in prayer, will be yours. (Mark 11:22-25)

What God has done for me, he will do for you. It doesn't matter what storm you are facing in your life, God can handle it. He has already provided a divine solution for your situation. Your storm may be different than mine. You may not need a healing miracle. Instead, you may be challenged in another area; it may be financial or professional. Perhaps you've just lost your job. Your storm may be emotional, social or spiritual. Perhaps you're suffering from depression or maybe you are struggling in a relationship. Maybe your marriage is in trouble or you're wondering when you're going to meet your divine mate. Perhaps you're fighting an addiction.

It doesn't matter what your circumstances are, ***GOD IS A TURNAROUND GOD***! He can turn any situation around. Nothing is too big or too small. While you ("I") are in the midst of the storm, God is the ""I"" of the storm. He is the calm, the solution to whatever the problem or challenge. There is nothing God can't do! Absolutely, nothing is impossible for God when you apply your faith. Faith is believing in your heart, not doubting, praying, standing on God's Word and receiving your miracle.

I know because I am one of God's walking medical miracles. During the storm, my faith never wavered. I knew beyond a shadow of a doubt that God would heal and restore me. Romans 8:28 says, "All things work together for good to them that love the Lord and are called according to his purpose." I therefore, refused to believe or accept anything other than wholeness.

Today, I walk in complete health and wholeness. My body has been fully restored. Today, I am truly a picture of health! Look at God! He is so awesome! There is absolutely nothing impossible for God. If you have not experienced God for yourself, I encourage you this very moment to let go and let God take control of your life. He will bring you through every storm in your life. God has no respect of person. What God has done for me, God will do for you. I am a living witness that God is faithful. God will keep you safe through every single storm. God has promised that he will never ever leave you. God will bring you through and on the other side of the storm is victory...a rainbow in your life. To God be all the honor, all the glory and all the praise!! Hallelujah!!

"Thought For The Day"

"Every time I turn around, God is making a way."

Suggestions:

Keep a daily journal of at least five situations
God has turned around on your behalf.
Watch God show out or your behalf continuously!

Reflections

Reflections

Chapter Eight

Assured Victory Before the Storm

One day while I was reflecting on the events of the last sixteen months, I was directed by the Holy Spirit to read my journal entry dated September 12, 1997. I remember that day vividly because during my praise and worship time at home the Lord spoke to me in a vision and said,

> ***"Be still and know that I am God. Great and mighty things I have for you. Walk in faith. Don't look to the right or left. Stay focused on me no matter the situation. I'll give you peace in the midst of the storm, joy in the midst of the storm! I'll give you comfort in the midst of the storm. Joy...Joy...Joy overflowing in the midst of the storm! I will never leave you. Stay focused on me no matter the situation. I am God. I am moving you to a higher level for my glory. Let go and let me. Walk in faith. I have great and mighty things in store for you. I need you to say yes - Yes Lord. I know the plans I have for you. Just let go and let me. Keep a journal. I will show you. I will do exceedingly abundantly above all you could ever think or imagine. I will give you perfect recall. Walk in faith!!!!"***

Look at God! One month prior to the attack on my body and spirit, God gave me a word before the storm to prepare and assure me of victory in the midst of the storm. Hallelujah! My God is so awesome!! He never allows you to go through the storm without preparation and the ability to stand! Amen.

Keys for God's Deliverance in your Storm

Self Help Study Guide

What to do when you find yourself in an unexpected storm:

1. Prior to a storm, you must develop a daily prayer life.
   Thessalonians 5:16 - 18 *Luke 18:1*

2. Put on the whole armor of God daily.
   Philippians 6:10 - 19

3. Let Go! Trust God. Totally depend on God.
   Proverb 3:5 *I Peter 5:7*

4. Feel your feelings. It is okay to cry!

5. What does God's Word say about your situation? Look up scriptures that address your storm.
   I Peter 1:25 *I John 5:14 - 15*
   I Peter 2:24 *3 John 2*

6. Speak the word only. Mediate on the word.
   Psalm 19:14 *Psalm 118:17* *Isaiah 54:17*
   Roman 4:17 *Proverbs 18:21* *Isaiah 53:5*
   Roman 4:21

7. Surround yourself with people that are completely sold out to the Lord. People that will stand in faith when you are weak.
   James 5:14 -16

8. Stand firm in faith. Your Faith will unlock God's miracle working power. Scripture examples:

A dead girl and a sick woman.

Mark 5:21 - 43
Luke 8:40 - 55

Jesus heals a paralyzed man.

Mark 2:1 - 5
Luke 5:17 - 20

9. Be a blessing to someone (Spiritual law of giving).
   Mark 4:24 - 25
   Luke 6:37 - 38

10. Know that you will be attacked as you approach victory. The enemy comes to take the word out of you by putting pressure on you.
    I Peter 5:8-11

11. Know that discouragement is of the devil.
    Resist the devil and he will flee.
    Laugh at the devil!
    James 4:7

12. Worship the Lord for who he is.
    I Thessalonians 5:17

13. Praise God in advance for the Victory.
    Victory in your praise and shout.
    Hebrew 13:15

My Favorite Scriptures During the Storm

Ephesians 3:20
Proverbs 3:5-6
Isaiah 54:10
Isaiah 54:17
Isaiah 55:11
Joshua 1:5
Jeremiah 29:11
Psalm 8
James 1:2-4
Luke 1:37
Luke 6:37-38
2 Timothy 1:7
I Corinthians 10:12-13

About the Author

Tracy R. Flaggs was born in Detroit, Michigan. She and her brother Brian were raised by their God-fearing, principle centered and loving Grandparents.

Ms. Flaggs accepted Christ as her personal savior at the early age of seven and she has a great love for Him. She is known for her faith, passion and love for people. She touches other lives with her inspiration and encouragement.

She is a multi-talented and dynamic person in both her professional career and in the work of the Lord. She is a lean manufacturing, logistics and supply chain management executive. Presently, Tracy is responsible for global transportation purchasing. She empowers her staff to meet and exceed company objectives while facilitating each employee's personal growth and development. She is very active in several community service organizations. It is her firm belief that the rent we pay for our time on this earth is service and giving.

Ms. Flaggs grew up spiritually and received a solid foundation for more than 30 years at Chapel Hill Missionary Baptist Church in Detroit, Michigan. She is now a member of Word of Faith International Christian Center (WOFICC), where she is actively involved in various ministries.

In 1997, Ms. Flaggs "suddenly" experienced several health challenges that have taken her to new levels in her walk with the Lord. Ms. Flaggs is a walking medical miracle and has been asked to share her testimony at several seminars across the country. Her message is one of sharing the promises of being totally dependent on the Lord in every area of your life.

Tracy's soul desire is to serve the Lord – her Daddy – and to do His perfect will!!!

Order Form

To share the truth of an awesome, on-time GOD with family, friends, health care professionals, people of faith and anyone caught in the eye of a storm, contact Tracy Flaggs at:

P.O. Box 1407
Novi, Michigan 48376-1407

www.faithworx@aol.com

I would like to order ___ copies of *Caught in the Eye of the Storm.*

My name is ______________________________

My address is ______________________________

City:______________________________

State:_______________ Zip:_______________

Phone:______________________________

Email:______________________________

Church/Organization:______________________________

Pastor/Contact:______________________________

Address:______________________________

City/State/Zip:______________________________

Phone: (   )______________________________

The cost per book is: $12.95	$ ________
Plus postage and shipping: $3.00	3.00
Please include 6% sales tax	________
Total	$ ________

Please send check or money order